the
Dog Days
of summer

by Kristi Mc(
illustrated by Linda

Harcou
SCHOOL PUBLISHERS

Printed in Mexico

ISBN 10: 0-15-351659-3
ISBN 13: 978-0-15-351659-7

Ordering Options
ISBN 10: 0-15-351215-6 (Grade 5 Advanced Collection)
ISBN 13: 978-0-15-351215-5 (Grade 5 Advanced Collection)
ISBN 10: 0-15-358152-2 (package of 5)
ISBN 13: 978-0-15-358152-6 (package of 5)

2 3 4 5 6 7 8 9 10   126   12 11 10 09 08 07

It was a hot August day. I needed a hiatus from this heat. I decided to walk from my house over to my friend Komal's house, and then we could go to the park together. Just then the phone rang. It was Mrs. Das, Komal's mother. She told me about a secret birthday present for Komal. However, the secret present had run away this morning! She described the "secret" for me and asked me to keep an eye out for it. I reassured her that I would help and keep the secret. "Mom," I called, "I'm going to get Komal and go to the park."

"Be safe, Nicole," she called after me.

I began my walk to the dolphin sprinkler park. I didn't know I had just embarked on a wild adventure. Nothing much happens in my neighborhood, so I was surprised when I turned the corner and saw a fire truck, lights flashing, and a ladder propped against a tree. A throng of people had gathered.

I ran into Komal who happened to be standing amongst the crowd. "What's going on?" I asked.

"Mrs. Marsh's cat is stuck in the tree," Komal said.

"That's nonsense," I said. "Cats don't get stuck in trees."

"Yeah, they do, all the time," he replied. He was always so convinced he was right.

"Have you ever seen a cat's skeleton in a tree?" I asked. He looked confused at first, but then I saw the beginnings of a smile.

"Hey," he said, "do you want to find the dog that made the cat climb up the tree?"

"Whose dog do you think it is?" I asked.

"Don't know," Komal replied. "I didn't see it."

"How are we going to find a dog when we don't know what it looks like?" I asked. I was always practical about my adventures.

"I don't know. I guess we'll just sense it."

"Let's go to the park and look," I suggested.

"Sounds like a plan," Komal agreed.

We headed toward the park. Komal and I were excited about looking for a dog, and we certainly didn't have to look too hard.

As soon as we got to the park, we went to the dolphin sprinkler. A friendly dog was running around and drinking water. His white, scraggly hair was soaking wet, and his pink skin was showing through. He looked more like a pig than a dog. I knew by Mrs. Das's description that I had located the missing present. I was elated but still had to keep my promise to Komal's mom.

Komal and I asked around, but nobody knew whose dog it was. The dog looked harmless, so Komal decided it would be our dog for the day. Komal loved dogs, and I agreed with his idea. We made a makeshift leash, but it really wasn't necessary because the dog just seemed to follow us.

After playing around for a while, we headed back to Komal's. Surprisingly, the firefighters were still trying to get that cat out of the tree. One firefighter was in a precarious position. He tried to hold the flailing, scratching, clawing cat while making his way down the ladder. Komal and I watched with interest. Our dog seemed interested, too.

Just as the firefighter handed Mrs. Marsh her cat, someone at the site announced, "Hey! That's the dog!" At that very moment, our makeshift leash failed. The dog saw the cat and bounded toward Mrs. Marsh. Mrs. Marsh's cat leaped from Mrs. Marsh's grasp and into the tree again.

As Mrs. Marsh's cat resumed her spot in the tree, Komal and I were feeling bad. Not only did the firefighters look annoyed as they began the rescue process all over again, but by this time, Animal Control had arrived and was ready to take our dog. At the sight of the truck, Komal looked like he was going to cry. It was unimaginable, but in the short time we had spent with the dog, Komal had really begun to care for it.

As Animal Control approached the dog, Komal burst into tears. "They're going to take him away, lock him in a cage, and we'll never see him again!" he said.

I thought Komal was being melodramatic, but he was really upset. That's when I made a decision. I pushed through the crowd to the bottom of the tree where the dog was jumping.

"Here, Pinky! Come on, boy!" I called.

"Strange name for a dog," said one of the onlookers.

The dog turned around, smiled at me, came running, and jumped right into my arms. "Don't take him away. He doesn't mean any harm. Really, he doesn't," I pleaded. "I know the dog's owner, and we will be sure he returns home safely." I could see a look of shock develop on Komal's face, but at least the tears had stopped.

All eyes were on me, including those of the firefighters. All of a sudden, one of the firefighters came around the back of the truck. "Nicole, is that you?" he said. I couldn't believe it! It was my old neighbor, Emilio. He had been like an uncle to me. I hadn't seen him for over a year, since my mom and I had moved after my parent's divorce. I ran over and gave him a big hug. Pinky, the name I made up with a second's notice, came right along.

"How are you doing?" Emilio asked. "I can't believe you know whose dog that is!"

I didn't respond to the second comment. "I'm good. Just trying to stay cool on such a hot day. How are you?"

Emilio told me about being a firefighter and how much he loved his job. He said he loved it with one exception— getting cats out of trees. His theory was that cats didn't want out, and I had to agree.

"How's your mother?" Emilio asked.

"She's good." I worried that he was going to ask to stop by our house to see her, and here I was with a dog that wasn't mine.

"Let me help you take Pinky to his home," Emilio offered. "It's my break, and I don't think that cat will ever come down with him here."

Panic set in. What was I going to do? I watched Komal play with the dog. Pinky was trying to kiss his face. Emilio was like an uncle, so I decided to be honest with him on our walk home. Komal was tagging along, more because of the dog than because of being my friend.

"Emilio, I have something to tell you," I whispered. "I do know who owns the dog, but I had to make up this extravagant story so that I wouldn't spoil Komal's birthday surprise. The dog ran away this morning. I'm trying to find a way to get him home to Mrs. Das and still conceal the secret. I just couldn't stand to see him taken away by that mean old dogcatcher. My friend Komal was crying and was sure Pinky was going to be gone forever."

Emilio laughed. "You've got yourself in quite a difficult situation," he said.

My mother appeared at the door as we approached my home. "Nicole, what is that dog doing here?" was the first question she asked.

"Mom, that's no way to treat Uncle Emilio," I said with a smile. I saw her expression change as she realized who was at the door with me.

Emilio smiled. "It's been a long time," he said. My mother forgot all about Pinky. She and Emilio were busy catching up. I suggested to Komal that we go to the backyard with the dog and play so that they could talk. We ran off with Pinky—the name had stuck.

When we returned to the front of the house, Emilio was walking down the steps. "I'm going to see you tomorrow, Nicole. Your mom's cooking us dinner, and I'm sure it will be gourmet food compared to what I usually eat." He paused for a moment. "Well, I've got to get back to work now saving that cat."

I had to get back to returning the dog. "What are we going to do?" I asked Komal. "Will your parents let you keep Pinky?"

"I doubt it," he said. "I have been asking for a dog for my birthday ever since I could speak. They haven't gotten one for me yet. I think it might be a lost cause."

"Isn't your birthday soon?" I asked.

"Yeah," Komal replied, "tomorrow!"

"Perfect timing!" I said as Komal shrugged his shoulders and gazed at the ground. He was defeated before he even tried. He bent down to pet Pinky who licked him all over. Komal looked like he was going to cry again. "I've got an idea! Let's go to your house," I said. Komal frowned. "Just play along. I'll do all the talking." I ran inside the house and quickly told my mother where I was headed. Then Komal and I were off.

When we approached Komal's house, his mom and his little sister were sitting on the stoop. I told Komal to just listen, and I would discuss the dog with his mom. He nervously agreed. "Hello, Mrs. Das." She was staring at the dog. Her eyes were as big as saucers.

I said with a twinkle in my eye, "I have this dog here, and I am going on vacation, and I can't take him with me. I was wondering whether it would be okay for Komal to look after him while I'm gone since he loves Pinky so much." At this point a smile broke out across her face. Next thing we knew, she was laughing.

"What's so funny, Mom?" Komal asked.

"You will do anything to get a dog, won't you, Komal?" Mrs. Das chuckled.

"What do you mean, Mom?" Komal asked.

"Komal," she was still chuckling heartily, "that's not Nicole's dog. I am sure about that." Komal suspiciously stared at me.

"What do you mean?" he asked again. "That's the dog your father and I adopted for you from the animal shelter," she said. "We asked your uncle to look after him until your birthday tomorrow. He escaped this morning. Your uncle has been looking for him everywhere. I called Nicole and told her to be on the lookout for your birthday surprise. You should thank her for keeping a secret and getting the dog home safely."

The expression on Komal's face was one of glee. He jumped up and down and hugged and kissed Pinky, who seemed to be just as excited as Komal. "Thanks for your help," Komal said to me.

"It's been quite a *dog* day!" I replied.

Think Critically

1. Use context clues to determine the meaning of *hiatus* on page 3.

2. What kind of person is Nicole?

3. What was the author's purpose in writing this story?

4. What do you think will happen next?

5. Which character is your favorite? Why?

 **Social Studies**

More on Parks Use the Internet or another library resource to learn more about national parks in the United States. Pick one park in particular and summarize your findings on it.

School-Home Connection Retell the story to a family member. Be sure to include all the twists and turns of the plot. Discuss whether you would have handled the situation the same way or differently than Nicole did.

Word Count: 1,794

GRADE 5

Lesson 17

WORD COUNT

1,794

GENRE

Realistic Fiction

LEVEL

See TG or go Online

 Harcourt Leveled Readers Online Database

ISBN-13: 978-0-15-351659-7
ISBN-10: 0-15-351659-3

The Dog Days of Summer

by Kristi McGee

illustrated by Linda Bronson

Harcourt
SCHOOL PUBLISHERS

The
Dog Days
of summer

by Kristi McGee
illustrated by Linda Bronson

SCHOOL PUBLISHERS

Printed in Mexico

ISBN 10: 0-15-351659-3
ISBN 13: 978-0-15-351659-7

Ordering Options
ISBN 10: 0-15-351215-6 (Grade 5 Advanced Collection)
ISBN 13: 978-0-15-351215-5 (Grade 5 Advanced Collection)
ISBN 10: 0-15-358152-2 (package of 5)
ISBN 13: 978-0-15-358152-6 (package of 5)

2 3 4 5 6 7 8 9 10   126   12 11 10 09 08 07